Big Muddy River of Stars

AKRON SERIES IN POETRY

Winner of the 2006 Akron Poetry Prize

AKRON SERIES IN POETRY
Elton Glaser, Editor

Barry Seiler, *The Waters of Forgetting*
Raeburn Miller, *The Comma After Love: Selected Poems of Raeburn Miller*
William Greenway, *How the Dead Bury the Dead*
Jon Davis, *Scrimmage of Appetite*
Anita Feng, *Internal Strategies*
Susan Yuzna, *Her Slender Dress*
Raeburn Miller, *The Collected Poems of Raeburn Miller*
Clare Rossini, *Winter Morning with Crow*
Barry Seiler, *Black Leaf*
William Greenway, *Simmer Dim*
Jeanne E. Clark, *Ohio Blue Tips*
Beckian Fritz Goldberg, *Never Be the Horse*
Marlys West, *Notes for a Late-Blooming Martyr*
Dennis Hinrichsen, *Detail from* The Garden of Earthly Delights
Susan Yuzna, *Pale Bird, Spouting Fire*
John Minczeski, *Circle Routes*
Barry Seiler, *Frozen Falls*
Elton Glaser and William Greenway, eds.,
I Have My Own Song for It: Modern Poems of Ohio
Melody Lacina, *Private Hunger*
George Bilgere, *The Good Kiss*
William Greenway, *Ascending Order*
Roger Mitchell, *Delicate Bait*
Lynn Powell, *The Zones of Paradise*
Dennis Hinrichsen, *Cage of Water*
Sharmila Voorakkara, *Fire Wheel*
Kurt Brown, Meg Kearney, Donna Reis, Estha Weiner,
Blues for Bill: A Tribute to William Matthews
Vern Rutsala, *How We Spent Our Time*
Clare Rossini, *Lingo*
Beckian Fritz Goldberg, *The Book of Accident*
Ashley Capps, *Mistaking the Sea for Green Fields*
Roger Mitchell, *Half/Mask*
Alison Pelegrin, *Big Muddy River of Stars*

Big Muddy River of Stars

Poems

Alison Pelegrin

The University of Akron Press
Akron, Ohio

Manufactured in the United States of America.
11 10 09 08 07 5 4 3 2 1
All inquiries and permission requests should be addressed to the Publisher, The University of Akron Press, Akron, Ohio 44325-1703.

LIBRARY OF CONGRESS CATALOGING-IN-PUBLICATION DATA
Pelegrin, Alison.
Big muddy river of stars : poems / Alison Pelegrin.
p. cm. — (Akron series in poetry)
"Winner of the 2006 Akron Poetry Prize"—T.p. verso.
ISBN 978-1-931968-49-2 (alk. paper)
I. Louisiana—Poetry. I. Title.
PS3566.E363B54 2007
811'.54—DC22

2007031673

The paper used in this publication meets the minimum requirements of American National Standard for Information Sciences—Permanence of Paper for Printed Library Materials, ANSI Z39.48–1984. ∞

Cover image: *Starry Night River Boat* by JK Schwehm
www.figstreet.com/studio

For Ben and Sam, my beamish boys.

Contents

Three

One

Alone, Drinking with the Tickfaw River

Featherweight lawn chair, cooler for a footrest,
and me a squatter on the landlord's dock
where bait stealers teased a thousand times a day
until rowdy boats and summer scared them deep.
Day and night I snoozed on the porch
beneath a filthy orbit of fan blades
to the opera of my neighbors fighting
and reconciling in the glow of stolen wattage.

I saw them swimming once. Maybe naked,
judging from their skittish talk, but the water
smeared their bodies' pale particulars.
It was just me and the Tickfaw River.
Me with the taste of a tin can in my mouth,
feeling no pain, lighting a cigarette backwards,
the Tickfaw tricking me closer and closer
with echoes and music out of nowhere.

Is it funny that I was too lit to notice
twenty-five orange yards of extension cord
stretching from my outlet, over the driveway shells,
to feed the hungry plug of their deep freezer?
Mother would have pitched a fit if she discovered
the stash of whiskey in the woodpile,
and my father wasn't laughing
if he looked down from his company of stars.

To a Lawn Jockey, Lines Written in Spring

Snappy pappy, deadweight, chess pawn capsized
    for the greater good, revenge is sweet as all sugarcane.
Who crashed the camp yesterday, three days early,
    but Slum Lord in the Suburban with his snotty kids,
the man above the mantle come alive? As for his
    intruded threshold, grill pit uprooted to the rental side,
me asleep in his hammock, why bother hide it?
    While he soaked up the scene, I said my back went out
the day before when I took a machete to those limp
    banana trees after a month of watching them rot.
As for the truth, the spine-twisting deed, pollen betrayed
    when I had hoped it would settle down and fill my tracks.
In other words, he noticed right off that you were gone,
    dragged, he guessed, and he guessed right,
from the horseshoe garden to the pier, then bombs away.
    His wife went nuts in her tennis whites, wailing over
her AWOL antique, one of a set. (That brother
    of yours is inside, on doorstep duty.) Offering
twenty bucks to the kid who could dive deep
    and swim strong enough to bring you back to light,
she harped on the legend of the faithful groom,
    Washington's not-a-slave-just-black stable boy
frozen in a statue pose, a one-of-a-kind tribute,
    turned nouveau riche pastiche, turned message bearer
to the underground looking to rest runaway slaves.
    Or anyway, that's what the junior league says.
I'm back to the mildewed hammock, pretending to read.
    Carpenter bees, the ones she lured with honey and then
spackled in the eaves, drill until the big house sings.

In Livingston Parish, Dreaming of Li Po

Li Po, this is your invite to the Prop Stop,
a honky-tonk unreachable except by boat
where we'd tether to a buoy and then, barefoot
or in flip-flops, tightrope across a rug of skiffs,
two weekenders not looking for trouble
but ready to battle any slurs the hicks unleash.
I keep samurai toothpicks and wine on hand,
though little news and nothing but wild company
brave the drawbridge to visit this distant post—
only a den of armadillos and dime-sized frogs
that answer to your moon. Once a man broke through
my yard with a wild turkey over his shoulder,
but he didn't stop to talk. I later heard he was
some houseboat squatter come ashore
who uprooted a travel trailer, leaving behind
an acre of shipyard squalor, red clay getaway
and all. Which reminds me—lose the topknot
and wear an orange vest. It's bow season,
and I fear a wild pig, or worse, will discover
you sleeping off pink zinfandel in the palmettos.
Always travel at night, in a swarm of mist.
If you send word, I'll take the four-wheeler
and meet you at the property line.

Banished Immortal

Once the monks look up and chant in unison
the nickname Banished Immortal,
you know you're headed for the record books,
even if only for allusions to drunkenness
here and there in the poems of friends.
Knowing well the world has its spies,
that someone may write, *Look at us—*
ten cups apiece and still sober, or, *Friend,*
twice now I've dreamt that I left you in sadness,
you better learn to be the life of the party,
the one always drunk but never sloppy,
aloof in a way that says, *I'm just a loner*
who draws a crowd, zoned out to chase a poem,
nothing personal. Li Po, imaginary friend,
the moon must get so bored with our routine—
poem or no poem, every night beginning
in a lawn chair and ending in the same spot.
Here I am again, my eyes watering over,
more and more dazed. You tell me don't lose hope.
No matter how far you drift
in the empty boat, you're always home
by morning. You always find a way back.

Wise Men Still Seek Him

(in lights above an outside nativity display)

Dixon, it's March and your nativity is stale.
The spotlight of your shotgun house
leaves the deer hungry, the woods blind dark at night.
You strangled the tree stumps, rooster's shed,
propane tank, school bus, woodpile, fishing poles,
lean-to, John Deere, and gravel drive with minilights.
Nobody in the trailer park understands.
Four months, and my prize dogs still whine
at that woodcut Santa humping up the slash pine
to the reindeer on your roof. You think that's cute?
The life-size musical wise-men lamps stooped
before the pigpen with their gifts of gold,
myrrh, and frankincense? And the Angel of the Lord
in glitter hotpants and a hotel robe strung high
as a convict in the heart-shaped leaves of the catalpa?
With so many lights criss-crossing your property,
an astronaut could spot this trailer park from space.
If the blink lights don't sink it, they'll name your boat
a star—*Bass Rat* or *Cirrhosis of the River.*
Wise man, you should wonder why passersby
can ignore your holiday display and gawk instead
at your family. Wife buffalo, a butcher of a son,
a girlchild bastard fat. Before she squats
in the manger bed, you'll have to travel to Boutte
after He Who Left Her in the Family Way,
knuckle and gun him to a haircut and a wedding day.

Homewrecker

You'll never see a diaper from me,
whether I'm the baby's daddy or not.
Just like your sister Janelle—on the pill
and suddenly knocked up. Giving it away,
seducing me with sobs to cover for
the river trash you're shacking with. Go on.
Go by your mama's and grow the little brat
on dumplings and venison gumbo.
Oh, to be a flea on the wall of your life!
I'd pay to pass through Killian again
and count the jokers you collect with three
in diapers and a job sweeping hair
at The Gossip Shop. You'll catch the breeze
of a thousand big rigs, I bet, dragging
those potluck kids across the tracks
to meet their relatives—no better than
a salesman with a suitcase full of junk.
This time the truth is better than my fantasy—
you sneaking home after a weekend spent
pussyfooting on Trey's pontoon boat
to find your clothes in garbage bags
and a vacant lot where our trailer used to be.
Around you, crew cut kids circle on their bikes,
all the while bolder as they pedal up the drive.
It would have been easier to throw you out,
but the prize for holding the harlot's card
is more than being oops-a-daisy pregnant.
It's stares that smack like sucker punches
everywhere you go. It's standstill time

and backstab talk sweating you through
errand trips to town. I hope you pass seasons
peering through fingerprints on glass
for the storm you know is coming and the man
you know ain't. Nothing but worries walking
in your mind. Well, worries and the thought
of me at the wheel steering our trailer
down the red clay drive and across Tickfaw River,
ringmaster leading the biggest elephant in the parade.
People thought it was a tornado—sirens,
and a double-wide speeding through the sky
to land a new life in Ascension Parish.
And really, where else could destiny deliver us?
Come Friday, I'll be sniffing out fresh meat
at the Bingo Palace while you hook up
with the first redneck to listen to your barstool lies.
I'll be swallowing the beekeeper's smoke,
feeding dogs off your grandmother's dishes,
bachelor again, and king of all,
until I find me a new queen, keep her
inside draping scarves over mismatched lamps.

Shaggy's Soul Food Open Soon, Said the Sign outside of Tallulah

I once had faith in this message hand-lettered
on the side of a vacant building.
Now I put my money on the wrecking ball.
Since the four-lane opened a half mile
off the strip, only Bubba Suds Laundry
and Free Junque, an antique shop, remain.
No music but the blues for Shaggy.
With no prep work and no mouths to feed,
Shaggy could be anywhere. He could be
piloting this reckless crop duster that dives
with a roar before rising to answer its shadow.
He could be cuffed to the chain gang
that picks the highway for its crop of trash,
or living at the motel between jobs.
You know the type. No matter what,
he's able to scrounge change for a Lotto ticket,
figuring one day he'll collect a windfall
of unlikely numbers. For now, it's hard luck
in the land of the lone gas station
that sells chicken wings and shotgun shells.
Land of the blind man with a harmonica
for a mouth. He breathes the blues
as if he were witness to what pains us most.
If he sent a postcard, the print would start out
square and get smaller, a diagram
of trumpet sound, the volume down.

Squeezers

There Is a Tie That Binds Us to Our Homes
—Bulldog Squeezers playing cards

Do not be angry that we call you brother.
Like us, when you push back from the card table
and head home to a broad whose voice
outsharps the piano's black keys all at once,
you're green, a chump to think a winning hand
can save a poor man before he sinks under.

Over and over, you push back from the card table,
but you never leave, in your mind the magic math,
the bluffs and bets, the blind luck you need to win big—
enough, at least, to scrap the van for a dualie, V-8.
The Dream of the Monster Truck is worth
another paycheck lost, another doghouse night,

another long ride home to the broad's cranky voice.
Longer than what seems right, you stay parked in the drive
and suck a long cinder on your cigarette
to the tune of a Catahoula barking up the fence.
Meanwhile, with dusk as a backdrop, springtime grows
like a sponge the color of a chemical spill.

The screen door trumps the piano's blackest key,
straining a moment before it slams. That's your call
to come in, wipe your feet, and sit at the table to eat
the calf brain omelet she's scraping from the pan.
Like a fish, you open your mouth, but no sound comes.
You douse the plate with hot sauce and eat until it's gone.

What a chump to think a winning hand is on the way,
to think the dog you keep on a run out back
licks your hand with affection. So dumb, this dog,
choking himself to yank a bit of slack from the lead,
that when you undid his collar and opened the gate
he ran only as far as the rut he paced while choking.

Save a poor man before he sinks under,
you pray to the toothy god of dice. Once more
you stick your neck out—*Save a poor man before he drowns.*
You squeeze them shut, the cards you've been dealt.
The dogs on back bite through the deck.
They fight the chain; the chain fights back.

Don't Worry, Spiders, I Keep House Casually—

—Issa, translated by Robert Hass

Will I never be finished with looking before I touch
    and holding every pants leg suspect,
        with typing Issa's poem on an index card—

Don't worry, spiders, I keep house casually—
    then Scotch taping it near Brown Recluse Central,
        hoping to fool them? They stayed. They multiplied,

and the bug man freaked out, so prolific in my attic
    were their fiddle backs and dust bunny webs.
        I followed suit, abandoning unmarked boxes

and karate gear galore when stuffing the U-Haul
    for a move back home, a thousand odes in mind
        banished by the prospect of a single stowaway.

What did I know, what could I do
    but evacuate and spread the fear? At first word
        of spider, my relations piled back into the Town Car

and drag raced it over oyster shells, gone before their faces
    came to in a Polaroid. My father—a loose tooth
        used to spook him—was the only one to help unpack,

working for lunch on a Thursday in the Year
of the Dragon, an ordinary Thursday that turned out
to be day one of his last year on earth. They say

a proper goodbye should last until the traveler
is out of sight, and I still see him waving
from the dock as shrimp boats idle past.

Lost in Betsy

Hurricane Betsy used to take the blame
for what my people lost or never had—
deed to the house, photographs, kamikaze
contraband smuggled into Gentilly
by way of an Iwo Jima ex-marine.
The Great Wall of China, in needlepoint,
framed: I thought it was all talk, like Betsy's water
rising quiet as the dark, until it woke the house
with hisses snuffed from candlewicks.
So hard to believe what was told: rooftop,
rescue by boat, Grandpa Hip in water
to his chest, pulling himself along
the chain link fence to a crippled neighbor.
Bigot Hip, of the hand-rolled cigarettes
and sleeveless undershirts, a collector
of trinkets blasted from the enemy dead—
bloodstained letters, and a deck of faces
bound with a leg of Adelaide's pantyhose.
This he saved from Betsy, and his purple hearts.
Forget all else, even the recipe cards
and the poodle that chewed its white curls pink.
Now we bring our pets when we packrat inland,
and his box of loot. Evacuation days,
we dream in shifts across the hotel beds,
paddling down memory lane, lost in the list

of close calls—water seeping in the rugs
or stopping at the bottom step, cars floating off
that were parked for safety on the neutral ground.
The Chevette was a perfectly good ride,
but I miss most Granny's Pisces macramé,
knotted blind, and from a box of Cracker Jack
the mood ring she always said would come to me.

Jackalope, Farewell

When Jess wears her kitten clothes to bed,
I hear wolves calling. They make me itch
and muffle the music she makes
begging me to sell my glitter boat
and put the money on a minivan.
By the time she starts dropping hints
about her mama's health gone bad,
I'm sniffing for blood on the air
and ready to chew off a foot.
I'm supposed to say it's fine,
but instead it fevers on my soul—
the thought of that woman
stirring the pot with her salt cooking,
her six-in-the-morning voice
edging me out of the kitchen with demands.
Before I walk the plank to exile
in what feels like cuckold cold,
I'll have to tear the antlers down
and bury my trophy fish at sea.
As for the jackalope, I don't know how
to make him disappear. Stuffed in a killer pose,
horns branched wide as a wishbone,
he reigns from the cedar mantle.
Snowshoes pace behind him,
waiting for ice. I dream of following,
of my tracks blurring as they fill with snow
that when you breathe it tastes like fire.
After a few beers, I see everything
for what it is, like I'm a wizard with a crystal ball,

my eye the moon over a world
of synthetic weather. I think
I see myself down there, but I'm not
moving—a mad dog chained
just tight enough to keep
the mailman safe.

Baby, You Don't Know My Mind

—Leadbelly

I wish you were a man with tits
and I your bearded lady. In bed,
we'd trick like circus lions.
I'd always have a black eye.
I wish we were trailer trash.
Behind on rent. One light ahead
of the repo man in a Cutlass Supreme.

Mad Dog, my main man, hair
shellacked, glossy as a game cock,
I could strip at the same club
where you take money at the door.
You'd tell me, *Put some Neosporin*
on my motorcycle burn. I can't resist
a little tattoo to match your scorpion.

Li Po at the Crawfish Boil

Because wine makes its own manners, Li Po
arrives uninvited in our backyard
while we cover the table with newspaper.
Worse than a horsefly he pesters us—
pokes a finger in the potato salad,
spies on the cooks around the boiling pot
counting off top secret tablespoons of spice.

We ask him to stay. Joker extraordinaire,
he stages a crawdad tragicomedy
then smiles to show us cavities of corn.
He plucks nonsense notes on the mandolin,
and he's dragon drunk by late afternoon.
The frogs sing, but Li Po doesn't listen.
He opens another beer with his teeth.

I wonder if we bore him or if he thinks
our twanging voices chime like raindrops
in an empty goblet. My mother-in-law
just can't shut up about snails in her roses—
every night she sets out a saucer of beer
for them to drown in. *Paradise!* he shouts.
To stay dead drunk and never sober up!

Pretending mosquitoes are no bother,
he stays beyond his welcome, long after
the lighting of the citronella candles.

Out past dark in the comfortable lawn chair,
he croaks poems about the moon in monotone.
He befriends a potted cactus, smokes his pipe,
hears calligraphy swish in the willow tree.

In the hours before midnight, Li Po offers
infinite libation to everything
on earth. I join him and tip a swallow
of café au lait to the puddle at his feet.
He finally says goodbye, but he takes small steps—
a slug sliming across the porch towards
the moon's face golden on a lake of beer.

Two

Letter of a Thousand Days

Lake Pontchartrain, Tchefuncte, Bogue Falaya—
I should be more like Li Po, half-drunk, squandering
the night's best verses to the Yangtze just because.
Dad, why can't I say that when I think of you
I also think of Time Life Books—*Mysteries of the Unknown,*
their commercials with a knack for interrupting,
midbrawl, our weekend ritual, The Old West
Movie Marathon? I know you remember how
the TV screen blinked black and then revealed
a teapot squealing while twins two states apart
each felt the burn. No such mind's eye sparked for you.
I was at a Christmas party, and as I time it, you were
Crossing the Great Waters while I listened to Charmaine Neville
do Jingle Bells, Satchmo-style. If the screen split here
in the movie of my life, it would show me singing along,
eating a shrimp as big as my finger, and elsewhere
you polishing the dance floor with your date
before staggering to a stranger's table like a desperado
slow on the draw, last taste of the vaquero life
wicked away by a barmaid-slash-flamenco dancer.
O to be a villager again, clueless to the enemy
crouched outside the rough-hewn walls,
daggers glinting. The happy villagers can't take a hint.
We're roasting a pig on an all-night spit,
singing the old songs. Only morning could be safer.
The audience knows better, though they keep mum
as tumbleweed, even while Li Po sets his paper armada afloat,
and while you soft-shoe the fandango, little knowing
you ride hard for that oasis the sun repeatedly erases.

Ballade of the Easy Broads

Mais où sont les neiges d'antan?
—Villon

Tell me where, in what barroom or strip joint,
Can I find Angelle again, batons aflame
Twenty feet high, or her cousin Tina
Who did kick splits between tequila shots?
Where's the mousy one, unremarkable
But for that ham of a tail—Chisesi's Pride—
Who rocked me in a monster truck?
Where are the easy girls I used to know?

Where's the fat girl with Bit-O-Honey skin,
Waitress in Daisy-dukes and disco skates,
Teen queen waving from the Pegasus-white
Hood of a Cadillac? Meow! That hellcat
Let Dennis up her slip and gave him the clap.
Oh Désirée, Déjunày, Crystal, and Monique—
All you loose women from drunken nights ago.
Where are the easy girls I used to know?

I'm dying of thirst. I feel my way home.
I stumble, and the drag queen steadies me.
When the blonde stopping traffic on Bourbon
Turned my way, I saw a villain's mustache—
But still I ached to grope up her kimono.
Heavenly Virgin, I pray, don't ignore
Your prodigal and lonely desperado.
Where are the easy girls I used to know?

Faded beauties, you few who answer me now
Have big thighs and a kid on each tit.
Where are your daughters? Somebody, quick—
Where are the easy girls I used to know?

Going to Hell

We go to church on Sundays just in case,
but we are going to hell. All of us
are headed for the crawfish pot,
hot as a seatbelt in summertime.
Just look at our eyes in pictures—
red as sirens above slot machines
that spit one copper token at a time.
Look at our feet—stomping on hands
as if every day were Mardi Gras. Angels with smirks
and coat hanger wings, we poke to the front.
We strut the streets, highstepping
through the cockroach crowds,
slurring names, poking fun, calling on
Jesus, Mary, and Joseph for little things
like blue doubloons and Zulu coconuts.
We feel so sure, we say it like a joke—
Going to hell! Going to hell!
A blister with cayenne pepper in it.
A cruise ship with all-night casinos.
My daddy's down there disco dancing,
time's dizzy orphan in a carnival of smoke.
You should have seen how we boozed
through his funeral, hawked at his nose
and his suit, how later we cracked his safe
and split the cash. One pinkie ring apiece.
The limerick we wrote for his epitaph,
I can't remember. I haven't been back since.
All night the riverboat ferries back

and forth over muddy waters. On board,
the high rollers are nervous, hunched over
pyramids of chips, though every hand
is aces, guaranteed. The dice
are weighted to show snake eyes.
You can't lose. The moon keeps score.
It knows you cheat. You win some more.

How to Deliver a Baby in a Taxicab

—Worst Case Scenario Survival Handbook

Houdini of rescues, you're overtrained for the apocalypse.
If you wanted, you could steal a car, sniff out a bomb,

conquer an inferno for the child still lost.
Sirens glare in every language in your dreams.

You wake from a blitzkrieg of killer bees,
suddenly aware of what to do if the feet come first.

Breech birth? An extra towel or two.
Otherwise, backwards babies—taxicab or tornado—

unfold as easily as origami swans.
Perhaps today, Tarzan, you'll wrestle the alligator

terrorizing City Park. Blade between your teeth,
you'll gasp and dive, and bystanders will suspect

it's your blood spreading an inkblot tide beneath the surface
of the lagoon until you rise triumphant and thump your chest.

But what if nothing happens? No quicksand,
cougars, acts of God. That circus clown is no assassin.

The alligator won't fight back.
In fact, the day's worst pestilence is rain,

and would-be murderers wander the streets
without thinking of the knives hidden in their boots.

Prodigal

Lifter of scarves and glitter lipstick,
    tearer of checks from Granny's pocketbook
and vanished from the trailer ever since—
    it's long lost Brandy, slut-cousin-on-the-rebound,
all around authoress of smut across our name.
    Crafty disappointerer, bastard-maker,
concealer of abortions and live births,
    ward of an unknown state, tongue kisser
and more of total strangers, street fighter
    with tooth-scarred knuckles and a Vaseline smile.
Fibber in the first degree, killer of time
    between rides, snatcher of what truck stop diners
leave on the plate, finder of clothes
    in other people's closets, kin absent so long
we sometimes forgot to light a candle.
    Girl once pretty sans the mean mouth
and blue tattoos looping ankle and wrist
    like monsters of the deep, girl now more like
a mug shot of that former self. Spent girl,
    zombie besprinkled with jailbait freckles,
smoker of generic cigarettes, out-of-the-blue
    arriverer on Thanksgiving Day who raided
the Percocet stash before she said hello,
    who dumped her trash bag of stuff on the stoop,
and wears blue jeans more dirt than denim.
    We promise not to hound you, Brandy, O wanderer
and pickpockets' patron saint. Remove your broken boots,
    stash that wad of bills elsewhere on your person,
and for tonight at least, rest in a fresh bed,
    O daughter, O spacer of Texas between us,
O hitchhiker too weary to lift a thumb.

Junkyard Dog

Looks like she found herself a junkyard dog.
He'll show her what a fine machine can do.
He's going to take her to the hot rod show
With muscle cars to match her cherry pout.

He's going to lift her dress and rub her down.
He's going to make her rumble steady low.
Looks like she found herself a junkyard dog
To show her what a fine machine can do.

To show he's strong and where her hands can go,
He'll ease the Viper down a dead end road.
He'll scrape her with beard kisses while she talks.
He'll drive her partway home, and then she'll walk.
Looks like she found herself a junkyard dog.

Tattoo Haiku

A titty pirate
with an eye patch and parrot
runs a hundred bucks.

★

I bet you never
met a geisha straddling
a gun as she does.

★

Be more specific.
The grim reaper comes rebel
or patriotic.

Go, Poem,

and stick it to my mother-in-law. Tell her
I think she's faking the broken foot, Velcro cast,
peg leg dragging through our spotlight dance,
everything. I knew she would wear that dress.
This is my wedding. In Utah. With Mormons.
But tight as I am stapled in this gown,
I can't heave-ho and smack her, much less
put to rest her second line umbrella.
The cameras are on, and so I smile
myself to death. I know when to make a toast.
Let's drink to us. It won't be long, old hag,
before the family men die of your henpecks.
You'll sail to the tropics on a cruise to grieve;
I'll say novenas that you die by shark.
If voodoo fails, I have a backup plan—
to The Home before you can lazy-daisy
S.O.S. on your needlepoint sampler.
So long, chicken lady. Spend your rest
of days wondering what I did with those dogs
of yours, sob stories all, the ones, before
all this, I swore to house no matter what.

The Ironworkers' Epitaph

This is for Gaynel Jackal's first husband,
the one she loved, who lost himself to distraction
on a routine weld and dropped like an anchor
from a peak of the Mississippi River Bridge,
electrical shock's marionette jangling
the long way down until he hit the water,
the commerce below him never pausing, not
the dredger spewing a fan of silt,
or the tugboats, or the patchwork of barges.

And for Mr. Jackson, the very black black
man, who once drove his spoke-wheel Cadillac
to the snowball stand and offered to pay
for everybody in line. From behind,
he was a black man in a baseball cap,
but if he moved—his hands or his face—all
was pink as a newborn mouse, except
his absent eyelids, and his lips—remade—
forced open in a constant, gold-tooth snarl.

Of them all, it's Chester I remember most,
who sharpened gates of iron fleur-de-lis
for fun. If you forget that, the picture
to keep is the one of Chester kneeling
in a confetti of sparks before his father's safe,
the man dead a week before anybody noticed.
No key, no combination, no other way
to get at the stash of worthless things inside,
like a pistol engraved *Mr. Berretta*.

Now Chester sleeps in a chair with that gun
bulging beneath the quilt that warms his legs.
Chester, commando of the switchblade,
who fastened bridges with the suicide kings
and squeezed into rooms as tight as overcoats.
The novices handed down tools, and they learned
by mimicry—the focused burn, the blue
heart of fire, the mirage within it
cascading, more water than the steel it marries.

Eat Nutria

This is different from pinching tails
and sucking the heads. I just can't swallow
what somebody who uses chicken necks for bait

will dump like fish guts overboard.
Seagulls ignore it, no crab will touch it in a trap,
and, if they were paid to take it, the Kleiberts

wouldn't feed it to the gators on their ranch.
Still, the famous gourmet swears
it's the next redfish. He says it in French.

What the chef in the soufflé hat doesn't say
is there's no hair on its tail, like a possum,
and no amount of remoulade can drown

the nutria's nickname—swamp rat—
or bleach its scythed, orange teeth.
Meanwhile, nutria chew through levee

and swamp, leaving saltwater rot behind them.
The mapmakers can't keep up. Every year
Louisiana shifts a little, disappears,

the shoreline shrinks back from fishing camps
like oyster dressing pulling from the pan.
Sheriff Harry Lee was right to okay

nutria for target practice. That first night,
his deputies went nuts blasting sawed-offs
at red eyes startled by the Q-beam fog.

Mostly they drowned, or bled out in the neutral ground,
or glutted the canals like bloated stepping stones.
But those cops—they wasted so many housecats

by mistake, the mayor called the whole thing off
in favor of a better way. Maybe a second line
would tease the swamp rat out of town?

There's a bounty out now—the state pays trappers
four bucks a pop, no questions asked.
You should see the pirogues. As they pole in

half sunk from a heavy day of traps, everybody
wants to help count the bounty, a string
of tails aimed in one direction to a swamp queen

with gray teeth gunning a big truck's diesel engine.
She smiles smoke; she doesn't exhale.
Her bumper sticker: *Nutria trappers get more tail.*

Muffuletta Night

On our first muffuletta night
since the storm, the deli
my people adore was closed.
We got together anyway,
not a muff in sight,
though they don't let on
they'd taken the ride
across the Causeway to my side,
down my street,
and didn't recognize the house.
We talk Lord have mercy
and what's left for my dead dad to do
except jolt awake, take a look
around, and fade out once again,
all of us bedside whispering
dirty jokes like before.
They don't ask me much,
but there's the way Chester
makes over my new book,
especially the poem that seems to tell
his story, uncapping his Knights
of Columbus pen for me to sign it.

Breaking Curfew with the Ancient Chinese Poet

drunk we lie down in empty hills,
heaven and earth our quilt and pillow.
—Li Po

If it weren't for poetry, you'd be so lame
against my knack for braiding cherry stems
with my tongue. You want me on your team so bad,
you're pitching stones like Romeo below my window—
won't I be your sidekick since I have a fake I.D.?
Just like a high school boy, the way you ask me out
then make like I'm invisible, shooting pool,
waiting for daiquiri number two to kick in.
And what good is a joker without his mate,
a sixteen-year-old fool enough to shimmy down
the trellis and flatfoot through the thorny bushes,
yes her only language. Yes, the moon's an eyelash.
Yes, Bourbon Street, and the strippers tease
at first because I'm a foot taller and we're both
wearing Chinaman pajamas. Relax, teacher,
and learn by watching how to swap with tourists—
kisses for Southern Comfort. We pass tallboys
and cigarettes around a circle of unnamed friends,
and I'm beyond caring that it's four A.M.
We should keep on, tallying flinches
from the silver mime over coffee and beignets.
Anything but home. One whiff of me,
and it'll be lockdown in the guest bedroom
with nothing for fun but childhood games,
all of them missing pieces. Two weeks
of Battleship, Yahtzee, and the doodles
in my notebook—Lady Po. A. Po. A. P.

Pharaoh Says

There was a sewing machine in my old bedroom
        where, until Katrina, stood paneling and shag carpet
like moss or a meadow up the stairs. Had I found
    ye olde fondue pot and Buddha bookends
before the demo crew relieved my mama's walls

of creeping mold, I'd be at peace, my heart aglow
        with the light of candle saints keeping watch
from hurricane lanterns in the blackout nights
    of my childhood, back when King Tut was on tour
in the Big Easy and my parents made a night of it,

dad all silk shirts and medallions and a dirty blond
        handlebar moustache, mom chubby in a peasant skirt,
her look saying, "Let's get this over with."
    Sure, he was once a king, but now he looks
like beef jerky, and his solid gold clothes

are over the top. Even then, I knew it was bad luck
        to sift a mummy from the sand. I knew they brought
a curse of scarabs. Maybe a drag show would be better.
    And when did Tutankhamen ever wear falsies
and glue a peacock's tail of sequins on his brow?

In the house of P. we always loved our drag,
        all the men did, something I learned young
spying on my parents' Copa Cabana bash,
    slowly gaining faith that Lola with her
man shoes and empty purse was my dad,

a lesson reinforced on Halloween and Mardi Gras,
            and later at cousin Zachary's dance recital
when the men of my tribe spoofed cheerleaders
    in a simple tap routine. I have it on tape,
yet another heirloom ruined when the water rose,

one of those junk drawer trinkets I hadn't thought about
            for years, though it was always nice to come across
things like my father's sand-colored business card
    with the sphinx on one side, *Pharaoh says*
Phuck You on the other, an icebreaker

he flashed when he got out of hand drinking
            Rusty Nails and left the restaurant with devilled eggs
in his pockets or a breadstick up his nose,
    swearing to keep Drambuie and scowling scotch at bay
after he slapped us or tore up the sand trap in a stupor.

The water rose, but hurricanes were fun back then—
            flashlight disco, mom raising our shoes to higher shelves
in the closet, and fondue, our lone survival food.
    Dad made King Tut shadows by the light of the sacred heart,
and Pharaoh said we would be safe, so we were.

A Prayer before Landfall

I didn't ask for strength. I asked for it not
to be the last night we risked mosquito gas
to watch the stars make perfect, dizzy sense.
I said to the television weatherman,
Please shave. How about some infomercials
in place of this hurricane churning nonstop
on the blue screen while I gas the car and pack.
How long to leave for? What about the cats?
Somehow the kids believe we leave tomorrow
for a real vacation, not a landlocked
motor lodge in Cleveland, Mississippi.
I took my last look. I saw the sky pines
shift from foot to foot in the outskirt winds,
and I said, let them do so without omen. Amen.

Three

Li Po after the Storm

Shake it off, Li Po. Wake up.
This time it's not funny
how the beer cans scatter as you rise,
hungover and holding out, wondering
how long cotton mouth and headstorm
will reign supreme. Every haunt
with a view of the river and the murky moon
I searched on my way out of town, but you
must have been pub crawling, sloppy drunk
in honor of hurricane letter K. I blamed
a catfish dinner at the Holiday Inn
in Mississippi for the floodlights
in my mind those nights, but it was the thought
of you fooling to an empty court,
hiding from high tides in the attic,
hatchet in one hand, Beaujolais in the other,
the rafters and the rooftop pressing close.
For sanity, for sleep, I tell myself
you kicked out a dormer window,
that together with the dime store looters
you make three. There's no sense leaving now.
Four days in, the streets are disbelief.
You strain your eyes. Outside,
worse than daylight,
the army hovers with their Chinooks
in surround sound just for spite.

Three Sheets

Not pissy or smashed, just a little warm
in the throat, with a pen in hand
and Li Po up on my shoulder
in miniature, a bookie angel taking bets
while I eavesdrop on the muses
arguing my fate behind closed doors.
Will it be the corkscrew path
of a merlot junkie with purple teeth,
or the calm of one word, then another,
maybe posterity, but probably
just a fitful tide of half-lines
worth remembering, something
for a facedown drunk to mutter
when consciousness dawns.

In Li Po's poems, the booze talk
matters to me most—exultation,
and tipsy leave-taking of a friend
in silence, with a pledge of unsent
letters telling all. What else?
There's a rumor of poems
drowned as quick as written
because of modesty and some deal
he made with the moon. But I know
the taste of recklessness,
and I think he set the poems
afloat because he was drunk.

I can see myself doing it—
prodigal waste, a fleet of paper boats
navigating the river of night,
all that longing and forgetfulness
shouted to the staggering sails.

Your Psychic Powers and How to Develop Them

So many questions for my crystal ball
since the Ouija went incommunicado—
that librarian with a midget sixth finger, a nub
on her southpaw, does she ever nibble it?
Pack a punch with her knuckle sandwich?
I'd like to know what possessed me to record
details from the far-off summer of my death—the blind
heat, dust on a shelf of leprechauns—
on a postcard I stuffed deep in a drawer,
same place Aunt Carol kept her pistol
with the inlaid handle. And that Reiki landlord
who had me stand in front of a bare wall
before she gave up the keys—I wonder what
she saw besides green glowing in my shadow?
What does it mean that I have been so drunk
I never found the bar again, that dive
where punk rockers popped the trunk of my car
and stole my brother's shoes? We laugh
about it now, but be sure I lied the next day
when he had to wear high tops with a coat and tie
to Grandpa Hip's funeral. Was it grief
or a flashback to last call and a frat boy decoding
my lifeline in the dark that made me steady
my hands on back of a pew? Too soon to tell
if he hit the bull's-eye with thirty-nine.
Even so, it squats on the horizon,
a smear, a smudge, a tickle in my foresight,
a phantom limb itching to hit the lights.

The Squatter's Almanac

Brother, tell me again
what was so funny about
the slideshow in your digital camera—
"zero dead" in Day Glo,
Dalmatian constellations
of wall-to-wall mold, close-up
of a maggoty bag of rice.
Who took this one of us
with your flophouse mattress,
soaked, half a ton, a sponge full of silt
to yank from your bedroom
to the mound outside?
Never will my back be right.

Never will I forgive that fall's horizon,
its ashen windowpanes,
the flood line, peephole-high,
stretching behind us like a prairie of rust.
Even now, when you cough
you say it smells like your house.

Every weekend you gutted
a little bit with the crowbar,
and always a step behind you
was your thief, working in daylight,
another starved animal grown bold.
He looted the trash pile.
He came inside and freed your place
of an aluminum ladder
and its replacement. Took the good

crowbar, wheelbarrow wheel,
a cactus, a Mason jar of coins.
He cleaned your bathtub,
then cleaned himself inside of it,
leaving few clues—wet wipes,
and a heap of painter's clothes
dropped to the floor
to double as a bathmat, I guess.

More dependable than your demo crew,
this thief of slim pickings.
And so today, as the red
trucks line Miles Drive
where your house number
is whitewashed on the curb,
I wonder if the bandito watched
the bulldozers do their business,
if he hid nearby, obscured by ditch weed,
as your house crumbled
with a musty thud, wondering
where he'd next be squatting,
much like you with your cat
and your one dry guitar.

Big Shot

Look at me—refugee, evacuee
prancing with rhinestone sandals
into my new world of Cleveland,
Mississippi, ready for the royal treatment
even at the hardware store
which I ambushed one morning
at the local man's hour of six
to score an 8,500-watt generator
without even asking the price,
ketchup-mustard gas cans, chainsaws,
a hunting knife with a compass
and a well for waterproof matches
in the handle, acres of blue tarps—
certainly everything I might need
in the wetlands once my home.
It took a half hour to add it up,
for background noise a fizz
of distress from the radio, but I
couldn't let it get me down.
I wanted to live, and so far
I was first in line. The Leflore
brothers took my money,
but otherwise good luck
picking up the check if you roll in
with Louisiana plates. On seeing mine,
they must have thought, as I did,
Mandeville *used to be* on the Lake.
Even at the laundromat

(we only brought three shirts apiece),
they set the dryers on for free,
and with her last dollar a lady bought me
a honey bun and a Big Shot soda
before offering to fold my clothes.

Mister Thirteen Feet

At breakfast in the hotel lobby,
my boys made a buddy, a pinch-hit pawpaw
who never tired of high fives or the thumb trick,
until his fisher's tan went gray, his eyes
barely afloat in his face, and like that
he became Mister Thirteen Feet from Chalmette.
Thirteen feet of water and sludge in the house,
to the second story windowsills,
and the pool house, boat, in smithereens.
His nephews, Broussards from St. Bernard,
sent the pictures. That was Thursday,
the same day the hotel turned him out.
Mister Thirteen Feet, his wife,
their fat dogs, and carpetbagger luggage,
where to next? The sportsman holding
the door open wide had been perched
since dawn on an ice chest throne
in the parking lot with his family.
So weary of the gypsy routine,
they said to the housekeepers
don't bother to change the sheets.
It was sad, I guess, but I don't
remember. We were five days in,
two days away from the boot ourselves,
two days away from first word
of our pawpaw, Bruce, who squandered
precious gas—eighty miles to a phone

in service—to say he was surviving
and to stay away. No time for questions,
no time to pass the phone around.
When the operator interrupted the call,
that's when he broke the news about our place.

Mysterious Ways

He actually said it—that, and
Material things can be replaced.
Loud as a stump grinder, twice
he yelled from across the street
before I made landfall and was
out of the car to witness
the mess firsthand—three trees
through the roof, the woods inside,
and all our attic treasures crushed.
Ghost in my own house,
I passed through the wall
that used to be a wall, and he followed,
held the power lines aside.
One thing I recognized, unearthed
by the storm indoors, was my copy
of Catullus, trans. Charles Martin,
that once belonged to Ellen Gilchrist.
I bought it at a used bookstore
back when I thought it meant something
for a book to call me from the shelf
and then fall open to a page
she had marked with a scrap—
Remarkable, the way you go on living
with neither sweat nor spittle.
What I wouldn't give for a poet
as a neighbor instead of this
Southern Baptist thorn in my side.
He calls himself untouched, passed over.
I call him Sisyphus of the South,
dumping endless pine needles into bags,
red as the devil, pitchfork and all.

Night Thoughts

No plans for tonight but to snare a poem,
to set a breadcrumb trail of booze
and catch a little buzz myself. No big deal.
The kids are sleeping, and I'm straight enough
to hear the phone or get us out in case
of fire. I'm starting off the Li Po way—
wine and the wide world—though my wine's
in a box and my world is more a snarl
of rusted bikes than moonlit wanderings.
I hear he'd brush a poem in crazy strokes
then toss it and start another, all night
racing no one or his drinking friend Tu Fu.
An August rain tiptoes through the pines,
but I won't write on that. Give me duende.
Give me life-or-death. I want a poem
to hack into your unsolved heart, a poem
so good you'll think I'm lying, you'll think
I stole it from a book and changed the name.

Choose Your Own Adventure

You know the book—the one you read in secret,
last on the rack at the paperback exchange.
The rattlesnake uncoiling as you thumb
the corner pages warns you're down the wrong path—
you've misread the horoscope, commandeered
the wrong scenario—you thought the stars
were saying "teach," but they meant "learn
to play the saxophone," or "hunt for trash
with petty criminals." Your choice now is to skip
ahead or dabble in the work of it, more and more
a god of thieves as the temperature rises.

Convict or not, come lunch you could snooze
in the shade, or break for the tree line and the refuge
you know must be written somewhere behind it—
a woodcutter's cottage where you read old papers
and drink milk still warm from the goat.
If the bloodhounds break your wretched sleep,
no matter—open the book to another page, to a day
in your life as a wife gone fat to pad herself
against the Mister's alligator boots,
or work as a miner and spend your last page
trapped, the water rising like a tide of ink.

Open the book again and you are here,
in the spot you started, a hunter unable
to recognize as his own the tracks he follows.
You stand there, the world's best dilettante,
part journeyman and part Quixote, posed
safari-style on a wildebeest crumpled by a blind shot.

Or scratch that and begin once more, *in medias res,*
as a cowgirl more freckled than her Appaloosa pony.
We'd skim the book in every combination
to find why she pauses here, at this desolate crossroads,
facing west to a barn full of shadows.

You Loot, We Shoot

After the hurricane,
after the hotel weeks of sharing beds
and washing dishes in the bathroom sink,
and a go-see of our house in ruins,
the thought sunk in and held
like shrimp boots in the muck—mother, brother,
husband, and two sons—nowhere to stay.
Many nights, my heart flashed
a mad pulse as I wove the loom of half-truths
that landed us a rental month to month.

In Beau Chêne, behind their upscale gates,
they wondered at us. Instead of smiling
as they swept their porches, the neighbors
aimed spray-painted plywood signs
our way: you loot, we shoot.
Overnight, the motion lights went up,
triggered by a breeze. Their dogs left turds.
All season, the charade unraveled,
and we four adults with a single key
bore their snubs, rearranged our cars—
eternally disordered, it seemed—
in the horseshoe drive.

Mornings I left for the hardware store,
or for work, and almost forgot
my temporary life, that I would return
at dusk, a suspect through the gates,
to a two-story brick with no welcome mat

and left-behind furnishings. We slept
on air mattresses in the workout room,
the Stairmaster a stand for my lamp
without a shade, and sometimes
downstairs, where it was cooler.

For Halloween, we went as hobos
elsewhere, to streets that welcomed us.
The kids rode trikes in the garage,
and I had myself convinced
that I could write a poem
in the formal dining room—
all sea foam and mirrors—
by pulling the toy piano bench
to the card table and turning my back
on the world outside.

Hair of the Dog

Rough morning, but nothing I can't manage
with a soft drink and a moment of silence.
In college, I stopped the shakes
with the dregs of a go-cup
watered down on the nightstand
before stumbling into the world of unread books.
Now I'm slick, mostly to class on time,
where I take roll and drone on about the Puritans.
My father was like this, and his father,
and his mother with her sleeping pills,
and so on and so on down both lines.
Every day as soon as the kids are asleep
begins the ritual raising of the glass
to the dead, offering libations to bad luck
with words and this stupid hurricane. What a chore.
At 3:09 A.M. when the merlot haze lifts off,
I stay put, the air bed stuck to my back,
and count squeaks from the ceiling fan.
I have nothing to offer the moon,
and to me the gray dawn is no marvel
as it burns off shadows in this house
that never lets me forget I am a guest,
courteous house heavy on the chintz
and self-help books, nothing inside
of them I wasn't born knowing.

FEMA Trailers, Moonlit Night

Without the never-ending game of hoops
that parts for passing cars, I barely recognize
my mama's street—tiled white, packed tight
with FEMA trailers up on cinder blocks.
Strolling to the corner store? No more.
Not with sidewalks cooling in the FEMA shade.
And no store. There and back with some French bread,
I'd spy on my neighbors from the curb,
them blessing the meal, and sometimes fighting.
Every night it was a different show,
and every day I played it off, as though
I hadn't seen the boys next door lifting weights,
daring cigarettes to burn out in their hands.
Post-Katrina, it's their kids who cut up—
pissing curse words on the fence, gunshots
stuttering from their fingers at parked cars.
Only Ms. Vicki, matriarch, can bark them down.
Last week I tasted crab boil on the wind
and knew it was a Friday night in Lent,
which means boiled seafood served in her garage,
B.Y.O.B. Inside, under the bright
of a painter's light, she lets her grandkids,
any kids on rollerblades or skates,
orbit her living room stripped to the slab,
dodging stray nails and upturned bucket chairs.
If she had walls, the rigged-up disco ball
would cast a gray, no, silver streak of stars.
If she had walls, her cooking wouldn't be
a free-for-all, and I wouldn't hold my breath
when the planes dive close, spraying us and mosquitoes.

Thirteen Ways of Looking at a Jackalope

1

At a tag sale, rising from a hammock sea
with a dartboard star behind it,
the jackalope sticks its arms out: *Mama.*

2

Jackalopes in the wild, you never spot them.
They're still, like anthills,
and move only when the tumbleweed shivers.

3

This one's taller than all my books,
so I stand it on the curio shelf
beside the Blue Bird of Happiness.
Almost. It almost looks right.

4

Any taxidermist can tell you
how to make a dead thing
look alive. It's all about
choosing the right horns for the job.

5

The strangest thing—
rather than lucky sevens at the slot machine,
I see jackalope, jackalope, jackalope.

6

Windchimes bellow in the side yard.
The motion lights click on, but spot nothing.

7

There's the tale of the wolverine's disguise—
antlers fashioned from branches.
It crept to the watering hole
without spooking a single antelope.

8

In another story, the carnivore's horns
are made of wax, and they melt
when it huddles too close to the fire.

9

Jackalope is hungry.
My sons offer it grilled cheese and cat food.

10

The startled-looking shoulder mount,
the coonskin cap and tail-feather jewelry,
something in the hardware store
reminds me of home.

11

Postcard from Wyoming:
St. Francis of Assisi bushwhacking through the forest
on the back of a godzilla jackalope.

12

Jackalope wears dust like an outlaw's vest.
Spiders frame bizarre webs on his antlers.
Still, he needs something—
either fangs or a boutonniere.

13

Those pine trees you see
buffing the moon with paintbrush shadows—
look again.

Blue Roof Blues

I'm a lost soul standing where my house used to be.
Said I'm lost—where the seafood place used to be
Is nothing—no dumpster, no pilings, no speck of debris.

No Spanish moss to be found in a chain-link fence—
Instead of moss, you find sea grass woven in the fence.
In broad day, the shape of things doesn't make no sense.

Floodwaters left a stain on my shutters and doors,
On curtains and Sheetrock and shutters and doors.
The lucky ones can live up on the second floor.

There's a crop of blue roofs in some neighborhoods.
Rebuild or abandon—it depends on the neighborhood.
For a hint of the loss, drive the length of the flood.

The blue tarps blanket rooftops where holdouts waited.
Their attics weren't high enough, so they axed out, waited
For days, their names spelled with shoe polish just in case.

Yesterday I crossed the Mississippi to my mama's side.
Whole way over, blue roof blue in the corner of my eye.

Ode to Contractors Possessing Various Levels of Expertise

This one's a shout-out to the git-r-dones,
the crowd since Katrina most idolized
and sucked up to—seminude roofers,
hard hatters, electricians, tree doctors,
Ditch Witch pilots dwelling in tent cities
or, like our lumberjacks, the Dollar General
parking lot. A round of drinks and first pick
of the MREs for you. Look—one thing
I've learned is what you had to do, you did.
They roughed it, and my hubby pimped me when
he had me with my sweet voice make the calls.
Soon they came in pairs, like yin and yang,
one to chain-smoke in the truck, the other
to get paid—in our case, three grand up front
before Tangipahoa's understudies
of beanpole-rotund Rosencrantz and Guildenstern
would aim their crowbars at the fouled Sheetrock.
With no other prospects, we hired them
on the spot, feeling at once swindled
and spared on that first day and then the next
when nothing happened until dusk, and then
it came down all at once—skeleton walls
and Sheetrock ready to float before we could
line up shingles or a roofer. Sometimes
the vision doesn't translate to the page.
I'm not even sure I'm mad with them
for soaking brushes in my Calphalon
roasting pan and deciding we'd be fine

if they used the toilet as an ashtray.
Boys will be boys. They finished soon enough.
Maybe because we were nearing the end,
I liked the last ones best, Scientologists
out of Lafayette that we hired away
from a neighbor. I learned to barter with
this crew, longnecks for the long lost secrets
of the split-jamb door. We had a routine
going. Morning call at six in our kitchen,
coffee and chicory, kiss the shakes goodbye.
One day we had the photo albums out,
looking for a background shot of where
the plastered-over phone jack used to be.
Like children, like the rest, they moved along
and never call. A fiction, what I knew so well.
No proof but dirty thumbprints and memory
of their tattoos which slurred, "We're into knives."
A broken record, the blue lines of their body art—
dagger, dagger, dagger, dagger, heart.

Acknowledgments

I'd like to express my gratitude to the editors and staff of the following publications for supporting my poems before the poems became this book. *American Poetry Journal*: "Shaggy's Soul Food Open Soon, Said the Sign outside of Tallulah"; *Bayou*: "Wise Men Still Seek Him"; *Blackbird*: "Choose Your Own Adventure" and "How to Deliver a Baby in a Taxicab"; *Black Warrior Review*: "Li Po at the Crawfish Boil"; *Brilliant Corners*: "Blue Roof Blues"; *Burnside Review*: "Li Po after the Storm"; *Cave Wall*: "Don't Worry Spiders, I Keep House Casually," "Mr. Thirteen Feet," "Three Sheets," and "You Loot, We Shoot"; *Cimarron Review*: "Prodigal"; *Cincinnati Review*: "Hair of the Dog" and "The Squatter's Almanac"; *Measure*: "Night Thoughts"; *Ontario Review*: "Homewrecker"; *Ploughshares*: "In Livingston Parish, Dreaming of Li Po"; *Poems & Plays*: "Baby, You Don't Know My Mind"; *Poetry*: "Alone, Drinking with the Tickfaw River"; *Poetry Southeast*: "Go, Poem,"; *Red Mountain Review*: "Letter of a Thousand Days"; *River Styx*: "Big Shot," "Eat Nutria," "Going to Hell," and "To a Lawn Jockey, Lines Written in Spring"; *Shenandoah*: "Jackalope, Farewell"; *The Southern Review*: "Ballade of the Easy Broads," "FEMA Trailers, Moonlit Night," "Lost in Betsy," "Mysterious Ways," "Ode to Contractors Possessing Various Levels of Expertise," "Squeezers," and "Your Psychic Powers and How to Develop Them." "Breaking Curfew with the Ancient Chinese Poet" appeared in *The Bedside Guide to the No-Tell Motel: The Second Floor,* edited by Molly Arden and Reb Livingston (No Tell Books, 2007). Some of these poems appeared in *Squeezers,* a limited-edition chapbook from Frost Heaves Press (Manchester, 2005) and winner of the 2004 Concrete Wolf Chapbook Award.

A fellowship from the Louisiana Division of the Arts helped me to begin some of these poems, and summers off made possible by my husband, Bryan, helped me finish them. He has also more than once rearranged a house to allow me at least a corner of a room of my own for writing. More than ever I want to thank my Gretna people, who have always been supportive of my work, even if it meant not asking a lot of questions and staying out of the way. Everyone at the University of Akron Press has been wonderful, especially Elton Glaser. Thank you all.

About the Author

In addition to *Big Muddy River of Stars,* Alison Pelegrin is the author of *The Zydeco Tablets* (Word Press, 2002) as well as three chapbooks: *Squeezers* (Concrete Wolf, 2005), *Voodoo Lips* (Poems and Plays, 2002), and *Dancing with the One-Armed Man* (Slipstream, 2000). Her poems have been featured on *Poetry Daily* and *The Writer's Almanac,* and in dozens of literary journals such as *Poetry, Ploughshares, Shenandoah,* and *The Southern Review.* The recipient of fellowships from the Louisiana Division of the Arts and the NEA, she was a Tennessee Williams Scholar at the Sewanee Writers' Conference. She teaches English at Southeastern Louisiana University and lives in Mandeville, Louisiana with her family.